Koko's Kitten

by Dr. Francine Patterson

photographs by Dr. Ronald H. Cohn

SCHOLASTIC INC.

New York   Toronto   London   Auckland   Sydney

In memory of All Ball.

Acknowledgments

*We would like to thank
Grace Maccarone for her invaluable help
in the preparation of this book
and
Jean Feiwel, our editor, for
translating this idea into reality.*

ISBN 0-590-44425-5

35 34 33 32   6 7 8/0

Printed in the U.S.A.

"Soft good cat cat."
—Koko

An Introduction

WHAT do animals think about? Dr. Francine (Penny) Patterson wanted to know. In 1972 she began to teach a female gorilla named Koko how to communicate using the hand and body gestures of American Sign Language.

Three days before Koko's twelfth birthday, Dr. Patterson asked the gorilla what gift she wanted. Koko signed, "Cat." When a litter of three orphaned kittens was presented to her nearly one year later, Koko chose a tailless tabby and named him All Ball. The poignant story of their friendship unfolds on the pages that follow.

Koko's Kitten was originally published in 1985, and much has happened since then. Koko is now in her middle years. Dr. Patterson continues to teach, and Koko continues to learn. At present, Koko has a vocabulary of a thousand words. And she is being taught how to read: She can recognize symbols and identify words.

Noting Koko's desire for a baby, Dr. Patterson has been searching for a suitable mate for the gorilla, not at all an easy task. The Gorilla Foundation, which supported Koko and a male gorilla named Michael when this book was originally published, has acquired a third gorilla, Ndume (en-DOO-may), as a possible partner for Koko. As gorillas are in immediate danger of extinction, the foundation is building a preserve in Maui, Hawaii.

Over the years, Koko has gained celebrity. She has appeared on *Nova, Reading Rainbow, Mr. Rogers' Neighborhood, Day One, Dateline NBC,* and *48 Hours.* Koko has been featured in articles in *National Geographic, The New York Times Magazine,* and *The Wall Street Journal.* And her artwork has been shown in galleries in Hawaii and California and featured on the front page of *The New York Times.*

Koko's story continues to fascinate humans because Koko has become an ambassador for the entire nonhuman animal world. Koko tells us what she thinks and she tells us what she feels: happiness, anger, joy, grief, generosity, greed, love. Through her life story, Koko teaches us that every species deserves its space on earth and deserves to survive.

When we originally published *Koko's Kitten*, we felt privileged to be in a position to take this wonderful story to hundreds of thousands of children. Many years later, we are delighted that we can continue to introduce Koko to a new generation of young readers...a new generation that will learn to appreciate and protect the majestic species to which Koko belongs.

The Editors
1999

Koko can be visited at www.koko.org

One-year-old Koko.

preface

ANIMALS are capable of telling us about themselves —
if we can find the right way to ask them.

In 1971 I was working on my graduate-school
project — testing gibbons to see if they could recognize
themselves in mirrors. It was during my study at
the San Francisco Zoo that I first saw Koko. She was
just three months old and had been separated from
the other gorillas because of an illness. She was quite
sickly, and zoo officials were afraid she might die.
Koko needed someone to take care of her. She
needed a mother.

Around that same time, I attended a lecture about
a chimpanzee who learned how to communicate in
American Sign Language — ASL for short. ASL, used
by approximately three hundred thousand deaf

Americans, is a language in which hand, arm, body, and facial gestures represent words. After four-and-a-half years of instruction, the chimpanzee could sign one hundred thirty-two words. I was very impressed. I wanted to do that kind of work, too.

I asked the zoo director if I could work with Koko. At first, he said no. He was afraid that I would work with her for a few weeks and leave. That would be bad for the baby gorilla. When I told him that I was willing to spend four or five years with Koko, the zoo director gave his consent. I immediately changed my project. I would study the language abilities of animals with Koko as my subject. I would try to teach her sign language. It was the first time this kind of study had ever been attempted with a gorilla.

That was fourteen years ago. The language project that I began in 1972 has become my life's work. Today Koko knows about five hundred words and uses over one hundred different ones every day. She is able to communicate how she feels, what she wants, even who she is. When Koko was asked whether she was an animal or a person, Koko answered, "Fine animal gorilla."

Over the years, I have watched Koko grow up. As a scientist, I have documented every phase of her development. As a "parent," I have cared about and for her and I have been proud of her every accomplishment. There were many times that Koko surprised, enlightened, and inspired me, but nothing prepared me for how Koko reacted when a small, gray, tailless kitten came to live with us.

This is the story of Koko and her kitten, All Ball. It is a story in which Koko the gorilla tells us about herself in a language that expresses love, anger, sorrow, and joy.

Koko signs "cat."

KOKO's full name is Hanabi-Ko, which is Japanese for Fireworks Child. She was born on the Fourth of July. Every year, I have a party for Koko with cake, sparkling apple cider, and lots of presents.

Koko knows what birthdays are. When asked what she does on her birthday, Koko answered, "Eat, drink, (get) old."

Three days before Koko's party, I said, "I'm going shopping today. What do you want for your birthday?"

"Cereal there. Good there drink," Koko signed.

"But what presents do you want?" I asked.

"Cat," answered Koko.

Later, she repeated, "Cat, cat, cat."

Koko and Penny.

Koko signs "mad."

I wasn't surprised that Koko asked for a cat. I have been reading to Koko for many years and two of her favorite stories have been "Puss in Boots" and "The Three Little Kittens."

Koko gets very involved in the stories I read her. When reading the story of the three little kittens who lose their mittens, Koko sees that their mother is angry and that the kittens are crying.

"Mad," Koko signs.

Koko loves picture books. Gorilla books are her favorites. Cat books are next. She likes to go off on her own with a book to study the pictures and sign to herself.

On her birthday, I gave Koko the usual assortment of presents — apple juice, some special fruits and nuts, and a baby doll. I didn't want to give Koko a stuffed toy because I knew she'd eventually destroy it.

The only durable toy cat I could find was in a mail order catalogue and I ordered it right away. It was made of cement and covered with vinyl and black velvet. I chose it because it looked real and it was sturdy — gorilla-proof. The toy cat didn't arrive in time for Koko's birthday, so I decided to save it for Christmas.

In December, I made a list for Koko. I drew about twenty pictures — fruits, vegetables, nuts, dolls, combs, and blankets. Every year, Koko gets a stocking and lots of presents. She loves Christmas.

"What do you want for Christmas?" I asked as I showed Koko the pictures.

Koko carefully studied the booklet. Then she pointed to a doll, nuts — and a cat.

I bought Koko some nuts and a new doll. I wrapped the toy cat and put it with the rest of her presents.

On Christmas morning, Koko ate her cereal and opened her stocking. It was filled with nuts. Koko threw the nuts aside and went to her next present.

Koko unwrapped a doll.

"That stink," Koko signed.

Then came the velvet cat.

"That red," she signed.

Koko often uses the word red to express anger. Koko was very upset. She started running back and forth, banging on her walls. She was doing display charges past me. They were angry, angry charges.

It is natural for gorillas to display when frightened or in great danger. They run sideways, pound their chests, then go down on all fours, and run back and forth.

But this was Christmas, usually a happy day for Koko, and she was with people she loved.

Later in the day, Barbara, a friend who had known Koko since she was a baby gorilla, arrived.

"That looks like a black cat," Barbara said to Koko. "Would you show it to me?"

Koko did not answer. She pulled a blanket over her head.

"Could I see it?" Barbara asked.

Koko pulled a rag over the toy cat, then tossed it in the air. "Cat that," Koko signed.

"Please let me see it," said Barbara.

Koko gave her a toy dinosaur instead.

I finally understood Koko's strange behavior. She was unhappy with her Christmas present. I had made a mistake. Koko did not want a cement and velvet toy cat. Koko wanted a real cat. Koko wanted a pet.

The toy cat.

Things don't always happen quickly where we live. Every day is full of its own activities. So it was almost six months later when Karen, one of my assistants, arrived with three kittens. The kittens had been abandoned by their mother and raised by a dog, a Cairn terrier.

Karen showed the kittens to Koko.

"Love that," Koko signed.

As we showed Koko the kittens, she gave each one her blow test. When Koko meets a new animal or person, she blows in their face. I think she is trying to get a better scent. When she blows at a person, she expects them to blow back. Maybe she expected the kittens to blow back, too.

The first kitten was smoky gray and white. Koko's blow test took him by surprise. The second kitten was a tailless gray tabby. He was also startled by the blow test. The third kitten, a brown tabby, did not react at all.

After the blow test, Koko seemed to have made some judgments about the kittens.

"Which one do you want?" we asked.

"That," signed Koko, pointing to the tailless tabby.

Koko chooses the tabby.

I am not sure why Koko picked the gray tabby as her favorite. I never asked her. Perhaps it was because he didn't have a tail — a gorilla has no tail.

That night, all three kittens went home with Karen. Two days later, the kittens came back for another visit. Koko was happy to see them.

"Visit love tiger cat," Koko signed.

First she picked up the smoky gray and white one. Then Koko took the tailless tabby and carried him on her thigh. After a while, she pushed him up onto the back of her neck.

"Baby," Koko signed.

She cradled the tabby in her legs and examined its paws. Koko squeezed, and the tabby's claws came out.

"Cat do scratch," Koko signed. "Koko love."

"What will you name the kitty?" I asked.

"All Ball," Koko signed.

"Yes," I said. "Like a ball, he has no tail."

Ball stayed overnight as a visiting kitten. By the end of the week, Ball was a permanent member of our household.

Koko had her kitten at last.

For the first few weeks, Ball lived in my house. Every evening at six o'clock, I would take Ball to Koko's trailer for an evening visit. I carried the kitten in my pocket as I prepared Koko for bed. Koko soon grew accustomed to this routine.

"What happens at night?" I asked.

"All Ball," signed Koko.

"Right," I said. "Ball visits you at night."

When he was older, Ball snuck into Koko's trailer by himself. It worried me in the beginning. I did not know how Koko would treat the kitten unsupervised. As it turned out, Koko was always gentle. Ball was never afraid of her.

Kittens should not be separated from their mothers until they are at least six weeks old. Poor Ball was abandoned by his mother at birth, which might have accounted for some of his faults.

Ball was an unusual cat. He was very aggressive. He would go up to people and bite them for no reason. He would bite Koko, too.

"Cat bite. Obnoxious," Koko signed, but she never struck back.

Koko did not like to be scratched or bitten, but she loved Ball in spite of his naughty behavior.

"Tell me a story about Ball," I said.

"Koko love Ball," she signed.

Koko signs "love."

Koko tucks Ball in her thigh as she wipes her brow.

Koko carries Ball on her back — just like a gorilla baby.

Koko treated Ball as if he were her baby.

The very first time she picked him up, she tried to tuck him in her thigh. That's where mother gorillas put their infants. Older babies are carried on their mothers' backs. Koko tried this with Ball, too.

Koko was a good gorilla mother. She combed and petted Ball to keep him clean. She also examined his eyes, ears, and mouth to make sure he was healthy. It was Koko who discovered Ball's ear mites.

Ball was often a topic of conversation during Koko's lessons.

"Love visit," Koko signed when Ball and I arrived for a morning lesson.

"Ball," I said.

"Trouble," signed Koko. "Love."

Koko seemed to enjoy conversations about her kitten. This dialogue took place between Koko and a research assistant named Janet.

"I'll give you some grapes if you tell me about Ball, the cat," Janet said.

"Soft," Koko signed.

"What kind of animal is he?" Janet asked.

"Cat, cat, cat," Koko answered.

"Do you love Ball?"

"Soft, good cat cat," Koko signed.

In addition to sign language, art is another way I test Koko's perceptions. Ball lay with a green toy on an orange towel. I gave Koko a canvas and some paints and asked her to draw Ball. Koko had ten colors to choose from. First she picked black for Ball's body. Next she picked orange for the towel and green for the toy.

"What about Ball's eyes?" I asked.

Koko picked tan.

Ball poses for Koko.

Koko's painting of Ball.

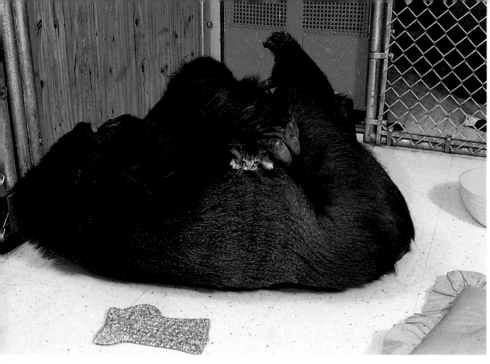

Koko tries to get a tickle.

Koko loves to play games. Her favorites are "chase," "blow-it," and "tickle."

Koko likes to be tickled, and she thinks that others will like it, too.

"Tickle," Koko signed to Ball when they were lying on the floor together.

Ball was not a good tickler, nor did he like to be tickled. So Koko and I pretended. I tickled Koko while carrying the kitten in my hand. Koko thought this was very funny.

"Chase, blow-it. Enjoy," Koko signed to Ball.

In blow-it, Koko blows as hard as she can into the face of her playmate. It's not hard to understand why this game was not one of Ball's favorites.

Chase is similar to tag. Players run back and forth and chase each other. This is a popular game among gorillas in the wild. But Ball never quite caught on to chase.

Koko did not realize that kittens don't necessarily enjoy gorilla games. Koko did understand that kittens like warmth, affection, and attention. And Koko supplied plenty.

Koko tickles Ball.

On a foggy December morning, one of the assistants told me that Ball had been hit by a car. He had died instantly.

I was shocked and unprepared. I didn't realize how attached I had grown to Ball, and I had no idea how the news would affect Koko. The kitten meant so much to her. He was Koko's baby.

I went to Koko at once. I told her that Ball had been hit by a car; she would not see him again.

Koko did not respond. I thought she didn't understand, so I left the trailer.

Ten minutes later, I heard Koko cry. It was her distress call — a loud, long series of high-pitched hoots.

I cried, too.

Three days later, Koko and I had a conversation about Ball.

"Do you want to talk about your kitty?" I asked.

"Cry," Koko signed.

"Can you tell me more about it?" I asked.

"Blind," she signed.

"We don't see him anymore, do we? What happened to your kitty?" I asked.

"Sleep cat," Koko signed.

A few weeks later, Koko saw a picture of a gray tabby who looked very much like Ball. She pointed to the picture and signed, "Cry, sad, frown."

It was an unhappy time.

Koko signs "sad."

Koko signs "red."

News of All Ball's death traveled quickly. We received thousands of letters. People of all ages wrote to us and expressed their sympathy. Some sent cards, others sent photographs, and many children created pictures. They all had one message: that Koko should have a new kitten.

As we approached Christmas, I wanted to get Koko a new kitten. I had no idea how difficult that would turn out to be.

On December 20, Barbara asked Koko, "What would you like for Christmas?"

"Cat cat tiger cat," was Koko's reply.

We heard of a Manx who was soon expecting a litter. We waited weeks until we discovered that the cat was just getting fat. Christmas came and went.

In January I showed Koko a picture of three kittens. One had a long tail, one had a short tail, and one was tailless.

"When you get another kitty, what kind would you like?" I asked.

"That," Koko signed as she pointed to the tailless cat.

"We'll get you a kitty like that," I said. "Is that okay?"

"Good. Nice," Koko answered.

"How do you feel about kitties?" I asked.

"Cat gorilla have visit," she signed. "Koko love."

Koko was ready for a new kitten if only I could find one.

More time went by. I called the Humane Society. They had no kittens at all — let alone a rare, tailless Manx. I called many other places and was disappointed again and again. I was told that not many kittens were born during that time of year.

The worst part of this period was my feeling that I was letting Koko down. I'd watch as someone would ask Koko, "Where's your cat?" And she would look around almost as if she were doing a double take, as if she were looking for Ball.

Koko's choices.

Then our luck changed. We received a letter from a breeder of Manx cats who wanted to help. He didn't have any kittens then, but he called other Manx breeders nearby until he located a litter of Manx kittens in Southern California. They were just about ready to leave their mother.

We set the date for March 17. The day before, I told Koko she was getting a new kitty — a red kitty. Red is Koko's favorite color. She was very excited.

Then, another delay.

The breeder called. "I'm sorry," he said. "The kitten is not coming today."

Koko was upset. I was disappointed.

"Trouble," she signed.

"We are having trouble getting you a new kitty. We have been trying very hard," I explained.

Finally, on March 24, a red, tiger-striped Manx was brought to our home. Seeing the kitten, Koko purred with pleasure. It was a wonderful moment. She placed him on her chest and petted him.

"Let me hold the kitty," I said.

But Koko would not let go. She kissed and cradled her kitten.

"Baby," she signed.

Koko was happy. Her new kitten had come to stay.

Koko feeds her new kitten, Lipstick.

epilogue

KOKO's "family" includes two other humans, Barbara Hiller and Ron Cohn, both officers of The Gorilla Foundation, and a male gorilla named Michael. Barbara is one of Koko's oldest friends. Ron is the photographer who has documented Project Koko from the start. He has acted as a father figure to Koko and Michael. Michael, who is two years younger than Koko, is like a brother to her. Michael has lived with us almost as long as Koko.

Every day at The Gorilla Foundation, Michael and Koko go through a regular routine that includes language instruction, review, exercise, meals, and play. Koko and Michael share a trailer that has been expanded and remodeled to serve the needs of two gorillas. Each gorilla has a kitchen, a small bedroom, and a big playroom. Out back is a fenced-in yard where the gorillas exercise and play. My house is only fifty feet away. I am always there when they need me.

Koko and Michael's education and care is provided through grants and contributions from members of The Gorilla Foundation. If you would like to help support this project, contributions may be sent to:
The Gorilla Foundation, P.O. Box 620530, Woodside, CA 94062